Meditative Poetry
A Spiritual Journey

On the Chariot of Stars
My Heart Flung Open

USHA DHUPA

BALBOA.PRESS
A DIVISION OF HAY HOUSE

Balboa Press books may be ordered through booksellers or by contacting:

Balboa Press
A Division of Hay House
1663 Liberty Drive
Bloomington, IN 47403
www.balboapress.com
844-682-1282

Authorized (King James) Version (AKJV)
KJV reproduced by permission of Cambridge University
Press, the Crown's patentee in the UK.

Print information available on the last page.

ISBN: 979-8-7652-3243-9 (sc)
ISBN: 979-8-7652-3244-6 (e)

Balboa Press rev. date: 08/17/2022

Dedication

To my Family of Teachers
Who teach me every day-
My four grandchildren
Whose blossoming lives
Radiate Joy.

It is a meditation on a way of life, and an examination of what happens when a life drifts from one continent to another. Uprooted and sprouted again in a new environment, in a different culture, in a new, or even in a similar environment and society, which you begin to view from a different prism.

Just like a myth, it finds its expression not only in a collection of stories, but in the beliefs, the ways and the lives that are influenced by the times that it is lived in.

Contents

Section III
God's Beauty Illuminates Existence

Section IV
Gathering Up the Petals

Foreword

It is my absolute pleasure to write the Foreword for Usha Dhupa's book, <u>Meditative Poetry: A Spiritual Journey.</u> I feel very fortunate to have known Dhupa for over twenty five years. Her gentle, loving personality envelops one in comforting warmth. I could not think of anyone better to write a book of poems dealing with spirituality.

Dhupa's <u>Meditative Poetry: A Spiritual Journey</u> Is a collection of poems divided into four Chapters. It starts with "Hymn of Creation", followed by "Dance is Life, Stillness is Love", followed by "God's Beauty Illuminates Existence", and ends with "Gathering up the Petals". The final conclusion is that all minds are part of one single consciousness, which is a part of Vedanta philosophy.

People meditate in a variety of ways, from prayer and yoga, to being one with nature. Dhupa shows that even writing poetry can be an act of meditation; it can help clear the mind and bring about inner balance. While some of the pieces in this anthology are very explicitly about meditation, others are more subtle, while some are meditations themselves.

Dhupa's entire life has been a spiritual experience. Her early childhood was spent in a pristine, spiritual setting in the Gurukul in Dehradun, India, in the foothills of the Himalayan mountain range. Even before that, she spent her childhood in the natural, almost primal environment of Kenya, in the wilderness, where she lived a simple and organic life in close proximity with the lions and other living creatures, with no delineated boundaries. Her father, a physician, worked there with a missionary zeal of doing good for the humanity, healing the sick and the wounded. She inherited this altruistic nature from her father, and every aspect of spirituality that she gathered into her soul was gleaned from these early experiences, and nurtured and developed throughout her life. In her poems, Dhupa has tried to show the salient aspects of life that bring forth the spiritual aspects of her life's journey. These poems are therefore a glimpse into her soul that Dhupa generously shares with her readers.

In her own words, Dhupa explains:

"To me spirituality in life is about trying to achieve a certain balance - to not get agitated, angry, depressed about things; to not get excited about good and beautiful things that happen to you."

She realizes that one is guided and protected by a force: in art, in life, in living and creating. Where is that force, that energy coming from?, she questions. The answer comes from within her: it is the consciousness of truth, love, beauty - Satyam, Shivam, Sundaram - the attributes of God inherent in a flower, in a dew-drop. In creation she sees a oneness of consciousness."

In short, Dhupa believes in the concept that the entire Universe exists in the formless God - Man, Nature, Sun, Moon the Stars - celestial objects as well as all the elements that give form and nourishment to nature and man. The joy, beauty and love in life are enhanced when Man is connected with God, along with God's Creation. (Section 11 and 111 of the book deal with the beauty and joy experienced in Life and in Nature.)

It is difficult for an average person to wrap his/her mind around spirituality. Like a friend guiding you, Dhupa demonstrates how she created her spiritual experience, which inspires the reader to do the same. Dhupa's poems are an open invitation to the uninitiated, as well as those advanced on the spiritual path alike to join her on her journey and experience the bliss and joy of all the spiritual gifts that can be gleaned from every aspect of life and nature all around us.

What I love about this book is how Dhupa has a very positive and comforting way of writing. This is what makes her book not only informative, but also entertaining and pleasurable to read.

This book is essential reading for any person desirous of understanding how to pursue a full and satisfying life. Her tone is heartfelt and her expression easily comprehensible. Her inherent message is useful and down to earth. There is much practical wisdom and guidance to be obtained from these pages.

Just as I have experienced great bliss in reading Dhupa's book, I invite the reader to share her joys of spiritual explorations.

In closing, I'd like to share a quote from the book which I found particularly heartwarming:

Filled in spirit with luminosity unrivalled
I gaze and gaze an'm uplifted
Skywards feeling like a feather
On the wisp of a wind!
With limbs outstretched, floating on an airy cushion
My past and the future become meaningless.

What is here is Now, and Me
With Infinity encircling around me.
In a protecting albumin, I am in the womb again
Viewing the world from my oyster-shell

Nourished and sustained
By life-blood of the Source of Life.

(From *WARM ENCASEMENT*

Section IV
"Gathering Up the Petals")

Meera Kumar Ph. D
San Diego
California
USA

Introduction

It is a joy for me to share with you my spiritual Journey – A Meditative Poetry: 'On the Chariot of Stars, My Heart Flung Open'.

My life opened up to the joy and beauty of Yoga postures, and recitations of Mantras from the Vedas at the age of five.

From five to fifteen, living in a 'Gurukul'–in an Aashram-like setting- in Dehradun, in the pristine environment, at the foot of Himalayas, in India, Nature was my classroom and playground.

With Yoga and Mantras at dawn and dusk - a canopy of clouds full of light above, and green mantel of deodars around, the full-throated, shrill voices of young girls kept the 'fire of eternity' alive. The Chanting of Vedic mantras reverberated in this place of worship.

Their poetic beauty and uplifting thoughts elevated minds to a spirit of devotion. The resultant calmness and serenity, the organic flow of life created an environment where minds were invigorated to absorb knowledge. In open air, under tall trees, surrounded by colorful fragrance of Hibiscus, Frangipani, myriads of songbirds playing in the background, Kalidas' beautiful poetry written in 4th century B.C. was consumed with as much relish as was the modern poems of Bachan or Mahadevi Varma.

The spirit and practice of these spiritual exercises and deep-breathing exercises generated tranquility all around, creating reflection, relaxation and wholeness in tender souls.

The oblations of fragrant, nourishing herbs purified the air with heavenly aromas, as clarified butter and camphor lit Fire in a large urn, the 'Havan Kund'.

The Fire a symbol of the Divine Light that perpetuates and nourishes life on earth.

A flower opens its heart to the sun and spreads its fragrance in all directions. The birds and bees synchronize to fulfil the divine intention of perpetuating joy of beauty and life.

When the heart and soul, in total embrace of the divine, feel awakened to the joy of the universe, the Spirit, in tranquil moments of awareness, enhances the spiritual dimension of life all around.

In meditative poetry, in an enchanting Spiritual Journey, we meet a world where the universe is alive, and imbued with subjectivity. It wants to live and breathe through you. When you see life in everything, you are on intimate terms with nature. The soul is awakened to a special joy, when the inner world is connected with the outer world.

Spiritual Living is self-awareness. It is the pleasant feeling of just being. A realization and awareness of the beauty, joy and peace that is meant to be pervasive in our inner life and in our outer life.

It is in the inner world of our spirit – the world of consciousness that we experience true love, joy and beauty that is inherent in the whole of creation. In Nature, there is a 'Oneness of Consciousness'.

With reading the poems slowly, listening to the rhythm of the heart, one feels a gentle tap of awakening to one's own life's precious moments. A triumph of the heart and mind!

While some of the pieces of this anthology are about meditation, others are more subtle, while some are pure meditations.

Free of Time Spirit floats carrying hopes of love, joy, and a devotion to the Supreme Spirit- the Light that gives Radiance to His whole Creation. Man's connection with that Core is renewed every dawn, when Nature is awakened to witness Creator's joy.

"Nature always wears the colors of Spirit: wrote Ralph Waldo Emersen.

Her poetry's delicate grace reminds us that life is rich, beauty is everywhere, and every personal connection is meaningful, and can have spiritual dimension. Our inner world connects with the outer world.

Love is the Primary Emotion that is pervasive throughout her poetry. Love of beauty and joy in Nature, Love of the Divine Spirit, along with the love in Human Relations.

In the poem 'On A Well-travelled Path' – the poet experiences a uniquely magical moment – when mind and soul are saturated with the marvel and the joy of the moment. "In that Moment of Being, we were fully alive, attuned to the miraculous event of the full moon, at close-up, a face -to -face encounter. Suffused with its 'Otherworldliness', we were one with the 'celestial body.'

In the spell of that moment, we were 'as a wave on the Infinite Ocean of Being'.

We stood there mesmerized, for what seemed like an eternity.

In retrospection, in that rare moment of mindfulness, our souls were 'bathed' in spiritual light.

W. B. Yeats wrote in 1912 that in Indian tradition, "poetry and religion are one and the same thing".

The yearnings of the heart and the soul often have a spiritual angle to it.

The Meditative Poetry: 'On the Chariot of Stars, My Heart Flung Open' is fully absorbed in the holiness of life, finding the spiritual in everyday life.

In, in a Spiritual Journey, in Section 11 "Dance is Life; Stillness is Love', we see glimpses of something very special, as mind opens up to self-discovery and self-awareness of life and life's celebration.

Tender loving emotions of a young expectant mother; fresh awakenings of love in a young heart – life is saturated with spiritual longings, and for life's yearnings for growth, and perpetuation of life's energies.

In 'The Love that Strung the Beads of Life', in the 'Tenderness of the Sword', we see Love reflected in a desire to fulfil its mission in life. Everything that serves man's spiritual needs is holy, thus purposeful for Spirit's enlightenment.

A heartwarming, inspiring book for the soul. The love, joy, beauty and godliness of her life's spiritual journey enlivens heart and mind, uplifts the spirit.

It is a 'Wonder' to be Experienced!

In these insightful warm personal narratives–aspects of her personal life, we witness spirituality in everyday life.

In living a life with mindfulness – with clarity and insight, she gives us a look into her personal Journey of Life. The enriching, meditative and spiritual experiences calm the mind, enrich the spirit.

Her joy in life, love, beauty and joy in life and in nature opens up the mind to new dimensions that we could explore in our own personal journeys.

Having garnered peace in the heart after cultivating right attitude to the presence of grace and beauty in life, we are able to capture the Joy of Existence.

In *Where the Spirit Soars*:

Ribbons of color floating in the breeze
Swinging, swaying with joyous ease.

In *Rivers Must Flow*:

In shrouded mystery
Clouded treasures of the begone
Trapped sunshine in frolicking rolling stones.

In *Trees*:

A small sprig, a tiny, pale promise of life
Sends a shiver of anticipation
A promise of leafy fan
Fresh robe for stern, bare branches
Seasonal delight, promise of light and
warmth!

with fragrance in the air; gurgling merriment in the waters;

Dancing rays in twinkling greens; Light bulb in a dew-drop in a leafy cup -

Nature is enkindled by spiritual fire!

In Creation, there is a Oneness of Consciousness.

*Even when life is lived with Divine Love at the center, there persists a lingering murmur, a constant simmering flame-in the heart. In solitude, in moments of tranquility and peace, it wishes to connect with the Divine.

In the ripeness of years, heart has a fervent desire, a longing to-merge in the Infinite.

Hence, the **Gathering up of the Petals**. A Final Celebration of Life!

A small drop, seeking an Infinitive Occan of Love!

Acknowledgements

First and foremost, I wish to pay a tribute to my gentle, loving Father and kind, compassionate Mother, who I grew to love so much, after being separated for ten years in my early childhood. Admired and adored, they are placed in the sacred altar in my heart.

With a missionary zeal to bring health and welfare to the sick and ailing in the frontier towns in Kenya, since 1929, they could not ignore their other equally strong passion – a commitment to Girls' Education. With great pain and sacrifice, they decided to send my sister Lata and I to India, when we were of ages of seven and five.

I am grateful that in choosing the Gurukul, at the foot of the Himalayas, in the spiritual setting in the abode of a 'Gurus' – the gentle committed 'teachers', and Yoga and Meditation, they gave a direction to my life of peace, joy and spirituality. It opened up a whole new world of wonders for me.

I greatly admire my dear husband Dhruv, whose exceptional talents of heart and soul, have enriched my life, beyond measure. Sixty years of togetherness have given me a new perspective on life. Reflections and emotions of the past and the present lives lived in two parallel universes, fill my heart with deep gratitude to the merciful bounties of the Supreme Lord of all Existence.

My heart goes out to our three children and four grandchildren, whose endless love and support has been a mainstay of our lives. Their joy in meeting with our inner lives, whenever lives' full calendar permits them, have provided me with the impetus to put a few thoughts together both in prose and poetry together.

My warmest thanks to Prof. Meera Kumar, PhD in English Literature. for her insightful comments in the 'Foreword'. Along with being a very talented artist in Indian Classical Music and singing, she has found fulfillment as a Professor of English Literature in San Diego, California.

I proudly acknowledge a very talented Mai-Lon Gittelsohn's leadership in guiding a warm group of writers through a maze of individual lives, from all over the world. In facilitating explorations of stories in a compassionate environment, in sharing the joys and hardships of individual lives, she has enriched souls of readers along with the writers.

I gratefully acknowledge the technical assistance and stewardship of Jannete Velez, in presenting the manuscript to Nick Salazar   of Balboa press, a Subsidiary of Hay House. Her proficiency and commitment, kept the venture on track. One could not ask for a better friend in matters large and small. Joel's expertise and availability at all the times of need was as welcome, as it was heart-warming.

My grateful thanks to Nick Salazar and Balboa Press, and Hay House

A FATHOMLESS, COLORLESS WHOLE

"In the calm of the mind, it is the substance of the mental being that is still, so still that nothing disturbs it. If thoughts or activities come, they do not arise at all out of the mind, but they come from outside and across the mind as a flight of birds crosses the sky in a windless air. It passes, disturbing nothing, leaving no trace. Even if a thousand images or the most violent events pass across it, the calm stillness remains as if the very texture of the mind were a substance of eternal and indestructible peace."

Yogi Aurobindo

Section 1

Hymn Of Creation

In the beginning
There was neither existence nor non-existence,
All this world was unmanifest energy...
The One breathed, without breath, by its own power
Nothing else was there...

Hymn of Creation:
The Rig Veda

AUM: The Universal Sound

*In the beginning was the Word,
and the Word was with God, and
the Word was God.
He was with God in the beginning
Through him all things were made;
without him nothing was
made that has been made.*

John 1:1-3

*This is what we hear about AUM:
The past, the present and the future are AUM,
And That beyond these three is also AUM.*

*It is unseen, transcendent, the sole
essence of the consciousness of the self,
the completion of the world."*

Mandukya Upanishad

On The Chariot of Stars

On the chariot of stars
My heart flung open
Gentle, tremulous, free.

Swinging, singing
Lucid light flowed
Throbbing veins
Radiant joy gorged

Sinewy wings
In ecstasy fluttered
A quiver in embrace
Motionless it speared
Drenched pure in ripples of Love
Deep immersed, it seared.

One, with One of
Luminous effulgence,
In sacred grove forlorn
Still, Blissful
Hallowed Radiance
Hailed voyager lone.

An Embryonic Breath

A vision beyond Light
From the *'Bindu',* it emanated
Expanded into rhythmic circles
Widened, overflowed
Into one immense Space
Of endless, seamless   *OM*

An all-embracing glow of Everlasting Music
A quest beyond edge, a thirst beyond satiation
In the Silence of the Mind
In the Expanse of the Universe
All-pervasive   *OM*

The Breath enveloped all
The All pervaded all
Nature, Man
The Universe Beyond!

From *'Shoonya' to 'Shoonya'*
It returneth,
Beyond – into infinity
It merges.

Into mute *'Bindu'*
A fathomless, colorless   *WHOLE.*

In The Stillness Of The Being

In the stillness of the Being
In the deepest, coolest core
The distances are covered
The dirt becomes pure.

Red Rose in the bushes
Far, far beyond
Beacons seeking heart
In kinship, joys galore.

Cold, warm winds converge
Ripples streak mirror ashore
Still tranquil budding glow
Refined gold chafed from ore.

A Vision Of Beyond

The shimmering echoes rolled on, anon
From wildflower waltz
to Infinite stars
From Seen to Unseen
To Visions of Beyond.

From sparkles and ambers
To Eternal Flame
The Everlasting Vibration
Sweet Resonance of AUM.

In the beginning there was desire,
which was the first seed of mind;
Sages, having meditated in their hearts,
have discovered by their wisdom
the connection of the existent
and the non-existent.

The Hymn of Creation, The Rig Veda

The Song of Dawn

Soft tinsel stirred the mute light
Misty veil blew over dawn's soft blush
In tender whisperings of awakening
Infant leaves brushed the breeze
Golden bristles swept the sky
rose-blush and gold.

Statuesque Aspens tall, demure
Dipped fresh in molten copper
Frieze the silver canopy high
Fleeting strokes streak the sky.

Entrenched in tranquil, pale light
My heart's stirring, like silver cloud
Blossomed, uplifted, expanded
Suffused in the peace of dawn
Into Oneness, it merged.

In the fold of Karunesh
The One of Love, of Compassion
It was All Love, as it awoke in
Surrender, harmony with Life.

Birds of Paradise sucked in the gold
Sang out vibrant melody aloud
Fleeting birds chirped, chirred
In quivering, concerted accord.

Flowing Bamboos, swinging, dancing
Welcomed enchanting life, in glow.
New day, conceived in morrows
Unfurled a promise of fresh dawn.

The Nascent Music

In my whorled ear
The sand-crusted shell
Echoes the nascent music
Jingle of a hundred bells.

Soothing heart in Mother's beat
Dulcet melody in invisible cord
The Ballad, the Bard in harmonious accord
Lyrical rhythm sweeps ashore.

Swimming joyful in cloak of Radiance
Floating, submerging in Ocean of Silence
In wholeness Perfection defined
The Maker, the Gem, play intertwined.

Liquid delight, cool, tender strokes
Caress the Core in blissful embrace
In ocean of Love, life-breath pours
An iridescent Pearl draped in silver robe.

Shrouded in Love, folded in Peace
The selfless Self births in deep repose.

The Becoming

On Goldsmith's atelier
In a sea of joy,
On a gentle palm
Lovingly kneaded,
Thoughtfully fashioned
In Father's image
Mother's loving visage,
Frolicked divine babe
Rapturous!

Eternity's white flag
Fluttered on music crests.
Crystal light in shimmering sprout
Heaved in joyous breast.

Pristine waters, radiant, pure
In rippling waves, spread ashore,
Divine breath on waters flowed.
Life, in perfection conceived,
In bliss matured.

Sushmina

Flashing fury, dazzling light
Fire in mysterious, indigo sky
Amid thunderous rolls
A spark kindled, of tender breath
In two glowing hearts gentle, devout.

She, the soul, burnished, radiant
Distilled in purity
Snuggled in heavenly fragrance
Bliss, Joy, Beauty divine
Sushmina, the Blessed One arrived.

Mother she is. The Birther, Nourisher, Sustainer
Love! Light of Love she is!
From womb to tomb, from birth to earth
All in one vessel
The Castle of Happiness – she is!

~My Piece Of The Sky~

A FAR-OFF HOME

Where the stars sing and tap dance,
The star-dust shimmers with a distant Hello,
The burning sharp-edged peaks of the Himalayas
The floating clouds of golden flame
Blazing and dissipating
Diffusing and blending,
Meet the gods,
I glimpse the primal dome
My far-off home.

A Hidden Landscape – My Inner World

A tiny spark awaiting a kindle
a speck of a seed fretting for green wings
a tiny cell seeking a match,
I had waited long, somewhere
in ether, in a mysterious space.

A warm flush of Love
in two sunny hearts
kindled the spark
alighted a Spirit.

A white fluid bubble, my soft massaging sack
cool, warm in synch with protective mantel
mother's nourishing chamber
A music box with tick-tock beat, gentle thumps
soft familiar murmurs
soothing, comforting rhythms.

The tiny molecule fed with
heavenly elements, earth, water
the seed nourished to a sprout
pushed through the warm earth
seeking the warmth of a light.

Snuggled in velvet smooth Vernix
I enter with a push and a thrust
blink hard in dazzling, harsh glare
strange thrum, deafening noise
my strange home, new, alien!

Lo! Gentle, Mystical Breath
breathes life into my blood
puny limbs kick and scream
seeking loving heart, nourishing touch
I swim in an ocean of cuddling waves.

A Twinkling Star In The Sky

I, a tiny starflower spurt out of
The fissure in the parched, crackling soil
I see a heavy raindrop sliding down
In slow motion

I am a fish with gaping mouth
To capture the raindrop.
The raindrops fill a lakebed
I am a Lotus happy, cheerful

Floating on an endless mass of water
That expands to a far-off horizon.
The horizon pushes up its fingers
To touch the stars.

I clutch those elongated fingers
Glide up the canopy
To be in company
Of the Evening Star.

Eternal Music

Fireflies shimmering in the dark
Elves dancing in the woods
There is music in the whisper
In the stillness of the Being.

Swaying Aspen heralding arrival
Conspiring leaves trembling in excitement
The hush of dawn
The first blush in the gossamer sky.

Life's blood ebbs and flows
In a rhythmic beat of the heart of the Universe
Endless, fathomless Creation's joy
Nourishing the sap if Nature and Man.

Joys profound, perpetual
Spilling into Eternity.

Man never to perish, never fading the bloom
Ever-humming bees never to swoon
The Lotus in embrace of itself
To close and enfold again and again.

Section II

DANCE IS LIFE,
STILLNESS IS LOVE

A New Beginning

A drop of watercolor paint
held at the tip of a sable brush by
no more than a few hairs
slid down the misty, liquid back and haunches
of the glistening white mare.
Her bristly mane fanned out in midair.

The drippy, gloomy night
was trying to shed off its veil.
The sun hiding behind blushing horizon
uncertain of its welcome.
It was a time when night and dawn
asserting their personalities
none victorious, neither willing to surrender.

In that misty, gray night, I saw
a dark apparition flying down from
the threatening clouds
getting brighter as it drew nearer
Two distinct streams of smoke trailed it.

I kept on painting
my large canvas capturing the welcome moment
of the arrival of the Warrior
The undulating figure in the distance was
like a Vision
I had long waited for!

The speck grew bigger and bigger
my picture grew larger, in proportion
As my gaze travelled between you and your image
each struggled to come out of the bleak night.

The distance grew shorter
the wings of your dark flowing robe
sheared through the clouds
You smoothly glided down
to land on a pool of slush.

My triumphant mare was smudged in mud
You, the Rider, an
Untainted, ethereal figure, stately, unruffled!

I kept on painting
the dew washing off the mud
The dawn was beginning to burst into a smile.

You took the brush from my hand
transformed the whole canvas into
brilliant hues of golden, crimson and pink!
Light radiated where there was gloom till now.

Your black shroud was gone
revealing a joyous Warrior
Proud and challenging
Ready to show his prowess
Gentle and strong.
It was a spectacle to behold!

The mud, the quagmire had vanished
You stood there luminous undaunted!

I, at once, realized you had come Home
This was going to be a 'New Beginning'!

Glimmer of hope uplifted my shoulders
Your radiant face revealed
A Smile in Victory!

Tenderness Of The Sword

The Beautiful Ancient Warrior
With intent, purposeful gaze
Fixed on the burning summit
Of frozen mountain haze
Embraces bright flame of Dawn.

The shimmering, lingering maze
Does not his stature faze.
His heart is besotted
By the image of Divine Maid.

Like a phantom, nay a Vision
She had awakened him from a dream
A life he had shrugged for so very long!

Like a Spirit of Light
She enters frozen heart
With a sweet incense
With a playful smile
An apparition from a world afar.

Like a melting wax
Around a burning candle
Her tender touch, ruby-red smile
Puts ablaze a yearning heart
Swirls around a heavy, thumping chest.

Swish-swash flashes in his mind
Thin flame running under his skin
The Spirit enkindled by Beauty of Joy
Fresh like the dew in the morn.

Life glows with live flame
The joyful bud of the heart
The flash enkindles brilliant resolve
A sparkling candle of Tender Love.

A River Song

Skip along, dance merrily
Trap the luster of sunshine
In the fullness of life
In its brilliant rounded lips.

Pebbles birth bubbles
Shiny shimmer trapped in eyes
Gurgle, murmur, singsong laughter
Rapturous joys.

Dark, mute night, steely slow current
Shroud of mystery!

Peals of laughter, soulful eyes
Shimmering treasures of beyond.

Tomorrows' new mornings
Potentialities, promises of bliss
Pristine dewdrops of ensnared twinkles
Brimful cups, full of nectar.

A Life's voyager
Diurnal click clocks
Tidal ebbs and flows
Journeys endless, unknown shores.

Meandering through endless vistas
In the depths of the ocean
We shall meet, all
In Oneness Beyond!

No identity, no shape
One with Elements
The wind-chiseled rocks
The water-licked smooth boulders!

The Love That Strung The Beads Of Life

On the pluck, the twang, the strum of Sitar
On the sweep of strings by Maestro's fingers
Two quivering hearts swung from crest of wave
To tremulous, shimmering, sonorous wake.

Pulsating melody bounced heart to heart
Pulling, binding, stringing together
Soft silken threads, woven in swirls
They intertwined in love, beauty, joy.

That love, the joy in symphonic rhapsody
It coursed a life its own
Rhythmic stream in sinews, in veins
Danced in vibrant liquid delight.

Strung taut, the heart-strings purred
Bound together they pulled, they twirled
The beads of silver, white and pink
Interlaced merrily with vibrant red and gold.

Wedding Procession

Shimmering, trembling Aspen
Greet one the other
Quivering arrows
Clasping hands
Whispering, gentle breaths
Fresh rosy Peonies of
Joys unstrained,
They greet in delight.

Life's joys await
Unknown mysteries to reveal
A vision of holy fragrance
Everlasting blooms.
A fount of gurgling spring
Cool, refreshing to sip, bathe in
A flight of pure white wings.

Dreams of joy, encompassed in eternity
Unabashed, unrestrained greeting
Of Time unfathomed!

Victorious, stately palms
Revered, serene pines
Acorns, pods and cocoons
Nestling grounds of form and spirit
Peaceful and serene
Cloistered, demure, mute.

Life's secrets enshrined
In silent tombs of perpetuity.
The warm womb of Mother Earth
In love and labor
Life to nurture and nourish
To spring forth again
In the mute smile of a Snowdrop.

Life greets life
With conjoined hands
In universal language.

A Dewdrop

Shimmering, quivering orb of pure light
On green crib, a light-bulb
Captured, captive, grounded in delight
Twinkling beams in ephemeral smile.

Capsuled in memory of the yonder
Nestled on a leafy cup radiant, malleable
A wondrous glimpse of pure heart
A reflection of the home from afar.

Rapturous joy lighting the flame
Infinity captured in brief fraction of the moment
Abundance of joy enshrined in time-capsule
In reverence, a homage to Providence's design.

I Hold A Flame

In my cupped hand, I hold a flame
The light that emanated at the birth of Creation
A bright spark, the kindle
The giver of life-breath
That perpetuates the genesis of Life

The Oak's womb, a warm, mothering Earth
The Cloud's gravity, in upward pull
The spurs move upwards, outwards, sideways
The greens fan fragrant, cooling air

Fruits of nourishment, seeds of life
The Earth, the Universe, united in purpose
Intention defined in conjoined hands
Life births anew, in the heart of the mother.

In The Folds Of My Desire

In the folds of my desire
Resides the Seed of Life.
It tiptoes stealthily into the recesses of my heart
Ready to step out on its tender toes
To scream its arrival, to whisper its smiles
To enchant the world with its alluring innocence.

From warm creases, springs forth a tiny spark
To enkindle, to warm up, to illuminate a yearning heart.

Layers of nacre dwell within the iridescent Pearl
Mysteries of Life enshrined in the labyrinths of the past.
The visible but a mirror
The reflection but a single dimension of the many folds
Encased in the golden shroud of eons.

Lifeless it never was
A treasure-trove of what was to become!

In That Hour Of Music

The sweet aroma, the cool spray of salty breeze
Swing on a drowsy, dreamy lullaby.
The inky dark furrows on the swaying ocean
Beacon to the horizon
That melts into the distant shore.
Orange, billowy clouds sing and dance
Around the crimson halo of the sun in eclipse.

I view a distant arena glowing in new welcome
To dulcet melody of soft, loving moonshine.

Resurgence Of Life

Surrounded by Shiva's resplendent light
The Shakti in me surfs on floats, on the waves of life
A rhythmic, gentle flow surges exciting anticipation.

My life's lotus opens up its eyes imperceptibly
Calmly the breeze sways, the petals unfurl
A burst of sunshine warms the heart, the limbs
Pads pedal wind in the sails.

I witness panoramic blue horizons.
Shakti swings on lusty waves, sings in sways
Floats on invisible cushions.
In a rhythmic dance
Shakti mimics the Dance of Creation.

Between peaks of the waves and deeps of the ridges
The Spirit floats in a turbulent gust.
It rises, it heaves;
It bursts, it sways;
It plunges, it surges upwards.
Limbs heaving with vitality
In Resurgence
It is Shiva in a Ring of Fire.
Iridescent, It images in Oyster's womb
Births the Pearl; forwards the movement of life.

Arms stretched; head thrust forward
To embrace the wind, the thunder, the thrust
The crushing Force!

To endure all with four strong arms
In a heaving chest, it absorbs the commotion.

Breathing out powerful conch of Victory
The resonance merges into the Flames of Life!

Shiva's ring of Fire illumines Life
Shakti's Grace perseveres
Leaps Life forward, into Eternity!

Motherhood

Rejoice!
Within you resides
The Breath of Life
The joy of Light!

A seed, a capsule
Infinite
Immeasurable potentialities
Of what is to be!

You an integral part
Of the becoming of it!

Body in preparation
Gradual, gentle receiver of
Knowledge of nurturing life
Inside of you, outside of you!

Tiny pearl
Mild irritant, discomfort
Acquiring layers and layers of nacre
Growing more radiant, Whole!

Nourished in a gentle mantle
Of mother's bosom, father's cozy palm
Fed by her lifeblood
Their timeless love!

In nurture is love
God's love manifest
In endless shapes and forms
In bounties of nature, body and soul!

Universal Soul
In creation, sustenance, preservation!

Father, Mother, the Universal Spirit
In love and labor
To create, nourish and preserve.

In creators of a miracle
Life's joys abound
Ever thankful
For Pain and Blissful all!

Soft Inland Murmur

Soft inland murmur
Melody tender and sweet
Lilting lullaby swaddled in light
Cradled in breath gentle, meek.

A gentle brook of nimble fleet
Soft treading pads of velvety feet
A lotus pure white, luminous, pristine
Sprung to light, smooth verdant crib

Into watery womb, rich, pure
Breath of life found home secure
Heart of the Universe in blossom displayed
Smiled in divine, sublime repose.

The Sea Shine

Snow-tipped peaks of morning clouds
Floating on pink, velvet sky
A herald of joyous delight
Mirth, laughter, sunshine, frolicking waves

Peals of laughter in pales of sand
Splashing, flashing limbs,
Tousled heads of pure delight
Pop up, disappear in watery depths
In thrills and chills
Boundless bursts of energy
In small, sapling frames.

The echoes of the ocean
Lullabies, glimpses into the Past
Depths, vastness unfathomable
Foreign land, wet land, watery- land
Out of element, yet of the Element
Fully at home, in a Foreign-land!

A Hill-Top Feeling Of Elation

I stood on a hillock
High and reverend - my five-year self.
Clouds descended
Faster than I could capture them
My little hands, my big arms
Stretched far and wide to hold them.

They floated around me
Hovered above me
Touching me, teasing me
Caressing me
Brushing against me,
Only to escape.

Folded in their gentle embrace
My tender frame enveloped
In silky cocoon
Their misty, wispy kiss softened my flesh
Wetness moistened my limbs
Oh, the cold, wet embrace!

I shivered, I quivered,
The joy of being alive
The pleasure of a tender embrace!

On A Well-Travelled Path

At sundown, one sultry summer eve bright
We bade Goodnight to a cooling crimson Orange
Sliding into steely-gray, corrugated Pacific Ocean
Of the Moon-light Beach.

In deep calm of unruffled minds
Thoughts and senses folded inwards
Wrapped up in peace and content
Dhruv and I entered D Street
To enrich the spirit, enlighten the mind.

On a well-travelled path
Turning into the Vulcan, the D Street
The lights of Encinitas Library on right
Beacons of anticipated joy of a special rite.

At a gentle incline of glistening, inky Asphalt
Winding, turning, snaking through shadows
We chanced upon a heavenly Sphere, massive, bright
A perfect round, an alloy of silver and gold
It halted our vision, had the sky
landed on the ground?

The earth and the sky, in one embrace
The far-away Roamer of night-skies
A shiny Platter, a shocker yet blissful
It had landed; still hung onto the silver sky
It laid there with a radiating smile.

To drive nearer, to touch, feel its satin-soft glow
Perchance, to scoop up the big, brilliant ball
We stood there in silence, in a timeless stare
The magic, the mystery engulfed, consumed us both.

Teasingly low, coyly it glided invisibly slow
Distancing slowly - Catch me, Catch me not
It frolicked with two tender hearts, child-like pure
Blushing pink with delight!

It stood there once, within arm's reach
A spill-over from the Day
The Queen of night, the brilliant Orb
It still glows two trusting hearts!

Marriage

A Symphony

Of highs and lows

    Love and toils

Tears and cheers

Waltzing

Cheek to cheek

    Hand in hand

In depths of rapture

Peers

Basking in the sun

    A dip in icy deeps

    Scaling arduous

Frigid mountains

Bruised!

Two inner compasses

One pivot

    Explorations

Oscillations

    Drums, gems, plumbs

And all

Rainbows in rain

Sunny

    Triumphant

In tears of togetherness

One

In fun and cheers

Never alone

In fears.

A Day Of The Feast

Canadian geese, Egyptian geese,
shimmering white swans
A flock landed on my shore, long before dawn.
The dark, floating cloud suspended in repose
Beside my Condo overlooking the lake.

The whiz, the buzz and clamor
Tumultuous shriek of flaps and clatter
Twirled around a few moments
Settling down in frenzied activity
The feet, the beaks hopped around in fury.

For regular sightings of migratory birds
The wind-chased bodies nourished
On greens of the lawn, on earthy worms
The algae in the waters, at lake's edge
Today was a Day of the Feast.

In the flurry and excitement on my shore
In rich shallow liquor, the evening before
Big and small fishes had enacted, to precision
A dance, choreographed in the web of creation.

In shallow still waters, nourishing, pure
Rich in algae, planktons, tiny creatures
The fish had congregated in numbers to spawn -
An impulse birthed, at life's dawn.

A pulsating mesh in lively dance
Swimming, swaying in water's cradle
New life heralded a feast for the guests
Searching lingering warmth, the flaming sun.

The internal map, the diurnal clock
Synchronized in cosmic design
Laid out, for a miraculous moment
A wondrous nascent event
I marveled, gazed upon!

The gong rang long before
The golden rays spangled glassy waters.
Frantic instinct in motion, Time froze.
The birds in single-mindedness
feasted till satiation.
The tables were empty
before the sundown glow.

I had chanced upon a brief moment in eternity -
Acted, reenacted, time and again.
The actors depart.
The show lives on!

Spring Everlasting

You keep on pouring
My vessel is never full
The eternal descending stream
from the Heavens
Never overflows my gaping urn.

The bubbling stream of Love
Twinkling Light in cool, clear waters
Scatters the beams that unfurl
The Lotus of my heart
Filled with ever-renewed joy
It blossoms in warm comfort
Fresh Hope unfurls
New Dawn of Beauty.
Each new day.

Section III

God's Beauty Illuminates Existence

The Bird Sings

Before the first light of Dawn
The moment of Yearning, of Intention, of Fruition
In the fluidity of Light, Hope is birthed
Penetrates the depths of the Night
With a gentle sweep of soft breeze.

The light spreads in rhythmic melody
Of colors, of luminosity
Orchestrated notes go afloat
In prolonged resonance of curtain calls
The joyful encore of bird songs!

Nature always wears
The colors of spirit:
Ralph W. Emersen

A Traveler From Beyond

I spy a raindrop crystal clear
In a verdant leafy cup
Shivering, quivering.
A glimpse of heart pure
Pulsating with life
Reflection of the Home---
A Traveler from Beyond!

A boundless drop
In a boundless sea!

A Reckoning

A small beat in the heart of the Universe
A tiny glint in a bubble
In many dimensions
In endless forms
Floating on a designed path.

Fragrance in a Rose
Sting in a bee
A chuckle, a crackle
Delights and moans
Relishes of laughter
Pangs of anguish
All in the Scheme of Life!

A web of myriad strands
Of rainbow-hues
Entrapped trappings
Rapturous labors
All of worth
All the reckonings
And all the mirth.

'Har Ki Porhi' – A Stairway To Godhead

Atop a rolling hill, overlooking a massive gorge in
the Himalayas, is the venerated image of a Hindu
High Priest, clothed in a white Indian robe of Dhoti
with a saffron scarf over his shoulders. On his bare
chest he wears a *'Rudraksh'* Jap mala – a Rosary of
one hundred and eight beads that are pods from a
holy Himalayan tree. In his left hand he holds a long,
white, silver-crested Conch, a Whelk from which
emanates the all-absorbing vibration- the prolonged
annunciation of Aum. A long-drawn Breath that
was but a Fraction-of-a-Moment at the 'Birth of
Creation'. I witness a slow unfurling of a 'Blossom'!
'First Breath' – Heart of Silence.
The vibration
The echoes of the vibration
The intermittent silences
That evoke the sensation of Eternity
The prolonging echo of the silences.
My hastened steps join the thumping flow of the
thrusting, crowding many. I, at once, become
one of the numbers who wanted to merge in the
harmonious Oneness of Humanity. As my feet
step on the first rung, a powerful boom of the
first Sound of Creation, the penetrating vibration
of ever-engulfing AUM, awakens me. My gaze
follows the large image of Shiva in the distance.

Nearer, it fixes on 'Har Ki Porhi',
the Stairway up to Godhead.
An enlivened populace in-waiting.
'The sound of the first cry of a new-
born', I say to myself later on.
To a mother, another birth on Earth
was just as precious and holy!

As the sound is amplified, the prolonged, powerful
vibration reached a crescendo as it seemed to
absorb us all into the womb of godhead. The
deep-throated, prolonged 'O' of wonder, followed
by the M, the mystery – merging into a womb-
like Wholeness. Lingering, submerging into a
fluid, calming echo of Silence – of: AUM.
Therein followed the *'Aarti'* – The Amazing Grace
in Sanskrit, extolling the attributes of the Supreme

Lord. The Omnipresent, Omniscient Creator
and Preserver of the Universe. The One Who
is *Bhu, Bhuva, Swaha* – The Creator, Protector
and Preserver- Brahma, Vishnu and Shiva.
The last one in the Trinity of Godhead, Shiva
embodies a duality. Shiva, the most venerated
of the Trinity of Godhead in Hinduism is a
benevolent God who is a preserver of life.
One, who brings an end to the physical
aspect of life – the sheath that embodies the
visible life-form, while the Non-perishable
Soul merges into the Universal Soul.
In a world where change and decay are 'inevitable',
Shiva's benevolence is expressed in his most
important role of 'Regeneration'. A Renewal,
a Regeneration into a new Life-form.

Hundreds of clay-lamps swing and sway on the
crystal-clear, undulating waters of the Ganges
gurgling, merrily singing! These puny vessels,
each with a flame, in a rhythmic dance pay
homage to the slow flow of the Ganga, as the
benevolent Shiva, the Meditating Yogi slows the
mighty rush of the pristine Ganga that has its
birth in the snow-clad Himalayas. The sacred
Ganges starts as meltwater from Gangotri Glacier
in the Indian state of Uttaranchal. It courses
through 1,557 miles of the fertile land of India,
in the end to merge with the Bay of Bengal.

The Mystic visualizes the protective Shiva in a
Meditative pose, at the Ganges's Source, as he holds
the forceful current of the river in his matted hair,
and mercifully releases its gentle flow to nourish
the grateful masses in the fertile plains of India.
Totally absorbed in the experience the devotees
connect with a life-giving force of nature - the
mighty, crystal-clear, pure Ganga, the Ganges
that nourishes bodies, and souls of a huge
section of the population of the world.
It also connects them to their ancestors,
whose ashes after Cremation, have become
part of the silt that enriches their holy land
that in turn nourishes the masses.
Broad green fields to golden
rolling hills surrounded by
waterfalls and streams cascade tranquilly into ponds.
It enhances the gratitude and reverence of the masses
for the blessings and bounty of spiritual and material
wealth that Mother Ganga has brought to their lives.

Fisherman's Net

In a brief moment of launching a flimsy vessel
challenging the might of deep, turbulent ocean winds
the coastline that loomed large is
soon vanishing into the distant horizon.

They drive vigorously towards the schools of fish.
Pounding hearts full of the thrill-
With the tinge of uncertainty
They glide over the Monsoon swept waters.

With the thrust, the sway
The lingering yearning to live, to perpetuate
The choppy oars of the color and
vigor of the frothy ocean
resound the tempo, the strength of the muscles and
sinews of the mighty men at sea.

The thrum, the drum, a harmonious,
perpetual heart-beat of the universe-
--Ho haya ho, haya ya, ho yaya.
Below the seas, above the ocean!

The wide net cast a semi-circular, irregular shadow
on the dipping sun in the western skies.
The spray reached the heavy, high clouds,
which responded with balanced thrust
Cast an equally wide net of heavy downpour
connected the inky, choppy waters
with the purple horizon,
the menacing, dark canopy above.

The wide sea allowed the fish to hop and leap!

In the Final act: the Heart of Surrender!

Hauling up a wire basket alive with flopping captives
Ho haya ho, haya ya, ho yaya!

A Misty Gaze

I am looking into my hidden valley
sliding down the asphalt, with a gray sky above
thickly wrapped up in sheer gauze.
I never realized that a gaze through the gauze could
meet such an impenetrable barrier.

Wait, a shaft of the morning sun is finally
piercing through the chink
where the wind's thrust has made a hole
for the light to creep in.

I see the view in the background;
and the ground becomes a visible part
of my environment.
The dry autumn leaves, brown, clumpy, crumpled
still lie on dirt floor
slowly becoming part of the earth
which had birthed big Oak trees.

The leaves, the trees, the earth
the sky, the air, the light
all the elements that surround me
wrap me in silent joy

I am part of all this elemental life
the life that I live today
and the life-form, I shall become tomorrow.

The noise of the world is slowly penetrating
the shield that the fog of my mind had
created around me.

I hear screeching of wheels
where the rubber meets the road.
Louder still, the sound of gravel
crackling under the tires
the children on way to school, chirpy, bouncing
bring in life, love, joy and laughter into my world.

The fast pace of life
the motor- bike with its powerful thrust
throws my inner world into the arms of
the rush and push of activity
that is another part of my life.

The silence of the mind
and the rattle of life
meet into a meaningful vocation:
Life and Life's Yearnings.

Feet In The Soil

Thump, thud, slush, splash
The heart throbbed; eyes smiled
A radiance of joy
Vibrant thrill of anticipation

A small inkling, a green sprout
Tall flowing grasses verdant green
Golden, rust-fruited crown
Earth's bounties poured over
Furrowed hands brown.

The wind song swayed, fluted in
Silver gray, frisky hair light
The heart glowed, swung on
Technicolor rainbow bright!

The Golden Haze Of Dawn

I opened the solid, wooden door
Peering into dense darkness
Cozily swaddled, wrapped in thick blanket
The day was deep, in dreamless sleep.
My flickering gaze, pierced the thick haze
No streak of silver lining, darkness to tease.

On total oblivion, beyond four walls,
I pushed the door back, soft and slow
Closing off sequestered peace, blissful repose.
In dim table light,
sleepy limbs stretched
To gentle Yoga postures, I breathed in deep
The stale air of trapped indoor breath.

In a world where peace prevails
To soft hymns of godly songs,
Shyly, ever so nimbly
Stealthily, the veil slipped.
Through a chink, a streak of silver
spanned the clouds
Embracing oneness, the sky
crept downwards to the grounds.

Mystifying trees, shrouding secrets in their folds
Went aglow with thrill, at the frill of their skirts
A breath stroke of color, panned radiant gold
The greens of the lawn, azure blues of the pool
Whites shimmering in gold, reds trembling in silver
Stirred slowly the mauves.
It was all smiles!

Trees

Where doth your joy come from?
What bard do you swing to?
Myriad melodies crouched in varied tunes
Bulbous, elongated; lime or deep, mysterious hues.

What secrets you hold, tender or bold?
Little chirps, squeaky, tender, shrill trills
Hungry mouths, trembling, quivering
A scream of joyous anticipation
A satiation of urge for survival!

Steely-gray sky, picture-less, blank canvass
Queer backdrop to joyous frames of summer
Massive, bold, proud or serene,
full-bodied or slender.
Bare limbs, crooked, ashen
Would whip the clouds away, if they could
Stoic, staid, moulds of endurance, patience and pride!

A small sprig, a tiny, pale promise of life
Sends a shiver of anticipation
A promise of leafy fan
Fresh robe for stern, bare branches
Seasonal delight, promise of light and warmth!

Parchment From Heaven

I hold the newly shed parchment,
the marvelously etched bark of the Blue Gum tree
am fascinated by its rugged edges,
eloquently designed
to tell a story of its fall from the smooth white trunk
standing bare in front of me!

life in perpetual need of renewal and regeneration
shedding off memories of the past.

In spite of its age-old memories of
the rain and the wind
the sun and the stars
the surface was amazingly smooth at a glance
while hiding some hidden chambers, at its core.

The inside of the parchment was like a new leaf.
What a wonderful design of ridges and rivulets
what varied hues and sinews!
A hidden treasure of lives' experiences encapsulated.

The veins that marked the flow of the sap of life
the smooth plateaus that clung
on to life and nourished'

protected the tree from the onslaughts
and vagaries of nature
and the cruel hand of man
a shield ensuring that life is sustained.

A wondrous, fragile cloak for a towering tree
pushing for a thrust into the heavens, after
fathoming the watery depths of mother earth!

Form And Spirit

Victorious stately Palms
Revered serene Pines
Acorns, pods and cocoons
Nestling grounds of form and spirit
Peaceful, serene
Cloistered, demure cathedrals.

Life's secrets enshrined
In silent vaults of perpetuity
The warm womb of earth
In love and labor
Life to nurture, to nourish

Glimpsed in
Pristine smile of a blushing bud!

It is in the aesthetic experience
of everyday life
That heaven and earth
come together.

Earth's Fragrance

A deep, expanding breath, to catch the mysterious,
earthy fragrance of the first Monsoon outburst!
The parched Earth, cracked, crackling
evokes layers upon layers of memories
of so many months of richly sensuous
enticing flavors and fragrances
permeates the air
enlivens the spirit.
The varied, ever-changing canvass
of Flora and Fauna in India!

An intense Earth Fragrance
as the Monsoon raindrops begin to fall
on parched soil
after five months of intense heat
that had saturated the soil with
an immense variety and quantity of
aromas of the rich vegetative life!

A distillation of the Fragrance of Life in India!

Where The Spirit Soars

Ribbons of color floating in the breeze
Swinging, swaying with joyous ease!

I am perched atop a seat-stone. Through its
deep crevice peeks out a surprise, a delight
for the heart, a bungee-lift for the soul!
A small, thorny 'artichoke', in vibrant, neon, bio-
florescent yellow color. A single soft - 'touch me,
if you please'! A heart-warming sunshine Flower!
Soft, gentle breeze, moving through fruiting citrus,
passes above heavy-laden avocado trees. Swinging
through purple Acacia- Golden Rain, it hums a
mellow tune in whiffs and gusts. Tinkling bamboo
jingles like lingering echoes of temple bells.
Scented Lemon Thyme or purple sage-
green, more Thymes ring carpets around the
walk of stepping-stones that carry my steady
feet to the arbors in terracotta color.
A field of golden Yarrow flowers, purples
of Mexican or Russian Sage, brilliant
white Azaleas feast the eye, and create
a soft wrap around my mind.
At a gentle incline, I find myself under a white
trellis. In variegated shades of mauve, the wisteria
creates a fragrant canopy above. So sweet and
relaxing that I often decide to embrace this

heavenly scent and linger a little longer to rest
on another convenient rock along the walk.
I strongly sense a divine presence, a fragrance in my
soul. Some intuitive wisdom, surely, had designed
this deeply personal and regionally reflective garden
of light, colors, sounds and aromatic flavors. A
delightful retreat in a valley of 'Olivenhain'!

Fully at ease, totally consumed by peace, I am
able to savor, to sip, breathe in and relish these
sensory delights of color form and function.
As I walk with Wisteria above, and the white
Gardenias, mauve and pink 'Sweet Peas' around
me, a heady aroma overpowers the senses – visual
and olfactory. The next moment, I am soothed
by the swinging tendrils of tender Wisteria that
come down to caress me with dew-soft petals
that tingle the flesh. I relish the rush of Joy. I
am consumed by the fragrance of Well-being!
Ahead of me, in the rosy, western noon sky, the
shafts of brilliant sunshine conjure up a large
shimmering star-twinkling among the sky-
hugging three Poplars. Rare for this naturally arid
environment of San Diego, these lush, green heart-
shaped leaves quake and flicker in gentle breeze
with internal light, shivering in the warm sunny air.
The breeze rustles, as a varied
musical soundtrack of birds,
the plaintive *'piyu, piyu'* of the
lovelorn Cuckoo Hawks
Enchant the Spirit!
A heavenly fragrance infuses the radiance of
Love, Beauty and Joy into my Core.
I am in a warm fold of: The sweet Light of Peace.
In my little Hermitage in the arbor
I Meditate on Divine Bliss!

~A Visitor From Another Shore~The White Bird

Low in the golden sky, I spy a graceful wide-winged
white bird, a heron, a Pelican, a Sea-gull shimmering
in the sultry breeze? Her yellow mouth, pointing
the direction with a narrow black beak, perfectly
matches the slender black legs with yellow talons.

Poised, she hovers over the cool greens of my
garden for a brief glimpse, and decides to land in
the clearing near the dry River-bed. A peaceful
sanctuary she has found in my garden, to hunt
for the rodents, to rest in the peaceful nestling-
ground. So different from her salty marshes or
mudflat habitats of San Diego's coastal wetlands,
or the Moonlight beach between the tides!

The cool greens and an abundance of shade
from the blistering heat of the noon, she spends
some time exploring her new home. She steps
on the walkway leading towards the bedroom,
as I stand there enjoying her presence in this
quiet peace of my garden of great diversity.

She must find some joy in the familiarity
of the palm trees of her other homes. Or
the Acacias of the far-off lands; perhaps the

shimmering, tall three Poplars remind her of
some distant land, in her annual sojourns.

She lingers in the cool environment for half an hour,
and for a better view, hoists into the air to perch
on the warm gray tiles on the roof of the Pergola.

At the click of my Camera, the graceful
ballerina fans her spritely wings, and in
shimmering joy, spirits away that heavenly
image, like a distant shooting star!

In my peaceful world, it is no small event,
when I am paid a seasonal visit by welcome
companions – the migratory birds in flight that
adorn the winter skies in Southern California.

On two consecutive winters, a pair of Egyptian Geese, on their migratory journey to the North, had spotted a 'large stretch of water'. A little piece of the Sea, they must have presumed, to have stop-over, for a day!

The next time, we were concerned, when the brown goose sat by the Pool, huddled up for full 32 hours, while the Gander sat close-by. The worms on the Lawn, the cool waters of the fall did not interest him!

With his mate fully recuperated, at the first flush of dawn, I saw two happy birds rise above my California Pepper trees, and shoot into the sky, to wherever their destination lay among the stars!

These special Visitors from the skies have enchanted us forever.

During our first year in the new house, while we were still making it cozier to embrace our first winter in San Diego, we had special visitations by diverse species of insects, butterflies and Moths.

One day, like a rush and push of a storm, we saw a huge colorful, flying magic carpet that dotted our near sky. The next moment, to our hearts' delight, we saw flashing green parrots with flat red beaks land on our two California Peppers in our western garden. For two consecutive years they too cheered our welcoming hearts. Their constant chatter and friskiness were something worth putting on record.

These joyful visitations herald seasons of color,
warmth and a new life of joyful anticipations.
During the nesting season of spring, doves,
sparrows, swallows, myriad new species of
birds, weave all shapes and sizes of nests
on the Poplars and the Acacias – creating
permanent seasonal homes for many species.

The Red-breasted Humming Birds, some with
flashes of green, more soft brown in shade, flash
by my shoulder or flit across my vision. Some
hover in my clear sight, their long-pointed beaks
dipping into the flowers of Butterfly Bush, the
Astro Marias, Birds of Paradise, even the surprise
blossoms of the Aloe Veras in Spring and Fall.

With nectar available the year around, Humming Birds are our permanent residents. Their welcome whizz past the ear or overhead, makes heads turn to view angels- fluttering, buzzing in clear view!

The white, yellow small butterflies, swarms of
Monarch Butterflies flying in from Mexico,
throngs of migrants on flight to rosier pastures,
or for perpetuation of the stream of new

life-forms, they hover over my sky. They stop awhile, to savor, to lounge, even to lay eggs for the next generation to perpetuate the lineage.

The evergreen, aromatic, colorful
garden is a home to many

Species that arrive to create new life cycles.

A constant stream of renewal of an
amazing diversity of Life!

Plumage

In the thicket of the Oak tree
Perched a Crown Bird
Waiting, waiting, waiting---
Huddled, scared, song-less
No home warm, secure.
The storm raged on unabated.

Glossy, clinging wings glued, cuddling
Warm wet solace, sole cloak.
Through dark night, deep in wet gloom
Warm hope in a cold breast nestles
Hovering, in a wet heart, heavy frame.

A ray of Hope
A spirit of strength
A promise of joyous morrow,
Piercing through the thicket
A glint of sun pours.

One eye, one wet eyelet peers
sees it all!
Hoping to dare, daring to hope
Dawn is here, warm and sure.
It chirps in faint, wet shrill trill
It will fly home, not yet---but soon.

Warm rush of Hope through wings of arrows
Fills the heart with swollen joy.
A thrust through clouds
Shearing, quivering flash, it goes---

Rivers Must Flow

Untold stories of yesteryear
Echoes of times gone beyond.

Dim folds in the sheen of light
Enshrined in frothy folds of delight
Wrapped in liquid satin, the brilliant gold.

Rumbling, tumbling gurgle in loud somersaults
Glistening bold rocks, flicked, lapped, rolled
Balls of brilliance, in meandering flows

In shrouded mystery
Clouded treasures of begone
Trapped sunshine in
Frolicking rolling orbs.

Spring

Spring leaves soft, translucent
Reflecting the morning sun
Tiptoe on the green foliage of yesteryear
They sway with joy of a new life.

Fresh and renewed,
Fulfilling the promise made to last fall
They swagger, they dance, the winds, the chimes
The music in their enchanting smiles

Hopes renewed, hearts frolic in joy, in love
Buttercups glorify the new-found warmth
Daffodils swing in melodious, flirty play
Earth rebirths in glorious, colorful display!

Summer

Firefly in summer's night
Trailing bright its dark path
Flits through the midnight charm
Its glow floating in whispering quiet.

Sun-touched kisses on Peach' flush
The seas swell for moonlight blush
Smiles bounce from one to all
Linger on, spread afar, on endless shores.

Autumn Winds

The autumn breeze chases
Leaves crisp, fragile on yellow floor
It played with trembling leaves
From branch to bramble as it flowed.

Crisp Maple leaves playing Ring O' Roses
Thrill and chill of sunset breeze in frolic
Golden, Crimson gleaming gauze, meek gaze
Shivering, shimmering in breezy delight.

Cooling rays of fading sun
In warm, coy embrace
Bracing, heralding a
Long-protracted Cold!

Winter

A lonely world of dancing shadows
Fall, spring, and winter meadows,
Shards of blue through bare limbs
Peeping, tweaking, far-off springs!

Glowing clouds, the blush of dawn
Shivering warmth of shimmering sun,
Shrieks of laughter tumbling joy
Shuffling feet through fluffy snow.

A lonely world of winter gloom
Hearths aglow, a smoky perfume,
Cherished, cherishing winter homes
Aloneness wrapped in shared domes.

Bonfires in luster,
Chestnuts in cluster
Splutter, splatter- crackling delight
Snowflakes, snowballs– a cheery sight!

Blue-breasted thrush, in chilled calls
Too-morrow, too-morrow, Hope intones.

R E N E W A L

Glistening, dewy fields of splattered hues
Dappled ribbons of greens, crimson and blues
Shimmering undulations far and beyond
Rolling, layered mounds of golden
Visions of plentitude - to savor, to behold.

Humming, swooning bees hovering
o'er cups of nectar
Bushy tails flicking, flashes in the arbor
Rustling, bristling haze, hides and seeks
Twits, trills, warbles, coos and thrills

Creeping, toiling creatures
In creating lush hills
Harbingers of life - in tunnels
Hollowed capsules, creepy homes
Carcasses, dung, juices of life that was
Remnants of past, nurturing
The Present and the Morrows.

Seedlings, sheathed in future dreams
Fluttering wings in mating dance
Synchronized, attuned to nature's plan
Fleeting flashes, agility encompassed
Joy perpetuated in dance of life.

Breath of sunshine
Whizzing through maze of trees
Brushing, caressing in kiss of life.
In worship, in love, life's joys pour
Brimful of nectar nourishing, secure.

Song Of The Wind

Mushrooms on my field
Staid, steady, firm and sure
Are Water Lilies in my pond

Dancing, singing
Flirting, swinging
Joyous, free, and pure.

Wind-washed, nodding in glee
Join me, come - dive in
They chant, and plea.

Life's delights free and pure
In forms welcoming and obscure
In abundance, pour evermore.

Section IV

Gathering Up the Petals

The Nightfall

When the screen above my fireplace
Has gone black, a Granite slate

The babe, deep in blissful sleep
Cushioned on mother's elongated neck

The toddler cozily tucked in with Father's
Tranquil, meditative self

I try to make sense of this moment
Of Stillness.

The Buddha, in deep silence of his heart
Studies the Peace, in the depths of his fold.

The Sun's brass coin dulled, slips away
As Sleep awakens to a world of Peace.

Slender Threads Of Life

To stay rooted in the moment
To hold on to my roots
To stick them deeper
into my consciousness
If no solid ground
to nourish me.

As I spread feelers
in all directions
Dangling to reach the ground
Fretting to reach skywards
I reach the Sap of life
Somewhere, somehow -

To keep me whole
To make me whole
True to myself
True to my place in the universe.

Slender threads of life
That nourish me
Nurture the Universe
Plug the holes
Where stars have fallen from.

To catch one of the stars
To put it back in the gap
Let me be there.

Let me be there
To fill up the gap with
Some fading constellation
Trying to catch up its last breath
To flicker just a little longer!

A Scaffold

A scaffold, a pinnacle
The in-betweens
One step
Then two
On a wooden ladder
Of
Faith
Insight
Keen Perception
Optimism
And
The resultant action.

Through The Open Window

The window was always open!
I blink, I discover
The soft golden light permeating
The whole length and breadth of the opening.

A glow, a radiance, that smoothened and soothed.
The ruffles, the creases ceased.
Two gigantic feet moved motionless, ceaselessly
Up and down, up and down
In a rhythmic flow, in a graceful dance
They floated on a cushion of timelessness---

The oceans churn, winds howl
Gigantic rolling waves move heavens and earth.
Giant footsteps tread invisibly
Only footprints are marked
Where they walked!

The substratum bursts into flames and fumes
Churning out gases, precious diamonds
In an unremitting effort.
It must rain fires and brimstones.
The Earth is made richer,
For giant, gentle Footprints!

The sun and the moon, heavenly constellations
Nurture with warmth and light.
What a splendid spectacle in the deep blue skies!

Mothers' breasts gorge to nourish the babes
Butterflies flutter across multi-hued fields
Bees swoon, giddy with incessant activity
Loaded with blissful water, the cumulus
Shower a bountiful rain.
Rainbows smile from rim to rim.
A peaceful sleep prevails.

The window is still ajar
I must not blink!

Divine footprints recall era
When Vishnu measured the sky
In three large steps

Warm Encasement

Atop a sand dune I lie
Naked to the warming elements
Blistering in pleasurable pain.
The sun-scorched crystals
Whip and lash the flesh
Eyes glued to cheeks
Escape the angry glaring ball.

There I lie. I live and breathe
A breath of glowing ambers.
Shining, shimmering sand
Burnished, crackling in piercing rays
Fragmented finer and finer still
All dust to the naked eye.

I lie on the sand dune,
Naked to the stars in the bright blue sky
Dazed at the marvel of being alive
Relishing my solitude.
The joy of the silent neighborliness
Of the vast blue vault above
Speckled with glimmering constellations
Swimming around the brilliant moon.

Filled in spirit with luminosity unrivalled
I gaze and gaze an'm uplifted
Skywards feeling like a feather
On the wisp of a wind!
With limbs outstretched, floating on an airy cushion
My past and the future become meaningless.

What is here is Now, and Me
With Infinity encircling around me.
In a protecting albumin, I am in the womb again
Viewing the world from my oyster-shell
Nourished and sustained
By life-blood of the Source of Life.

The warmth of glistening specks of sand
Envelopes me in its fold
To caress me with its undulating ripples.
I'm torn between what was on the ground
And what is beyond
in the tranquility of Grace
I muse;
I choose the warmth of an embrace.

~*Release*~

Cloistered in pearly cocoon
My silken yarn grows taller by the hour
Soft and strong, glimmering, shimmering
It knows not but to grow.

Hourglass tipping its weight
Something within me stirs
An urge beyond bounds
A nudge, a thrust, a gentle persistent push
And--
I escape!

Light as Ether
Shorn of garments of yore
Of yearnings, ambitions, holdings and treasures
On white wings, I rise
Lifted by a hand I have known only of Morn.

Tenderly, held on soft palm
In comfort, in peace
Devoid of shackles
Free!

Swaddled in tenderness
No pleasure, no pain; no joy, no gain.

It must be Heaven
If Heaven is bereft of chains!

My New Shore

On my misty shores, a gentle breeze blows
A glimpse of sweet promise, pearly opal glows

Blushing delight of bridal new day
Velvety petals swaddled in dew
Young sun piercing thro' violet haze
Beacons seeking heart, lost in maze

From my distant land, vibrant burst of joy
In songs of yesteryear, or some new tune coy
Melody enchanting, sublime, divine
To tender embrace, my heart is lured

Tall blue brushes, swinging rushes
Smashing rocks, pure joy gushes
New life stirring, heart-strings purring
In joyous surrender
I am secure.

Center Of The Circle: The Gathering Up

Three rings, four rings, five
Deep into the distance
Beyond tall dark trees
Beyond the gurgles of the stream

The chirps, the twitters
Crackling, decaying, dried leaves
Autumn is calling, I thought
But Fall has come and gone!

This is a call of Repose, of peace
Of introspection, of seclusion.
The annual call of winding down
To complete the circle.

The Spring of Birth
To the long, silent
Mystical, mystifying
Slumber of Death.

The Gong still calls
Another day, day after day
Another time, one more summer
A season of splendor.

Then the dark moon
Exhaustion of the borrowed glow
The sunset in distant horizon
Into mute retreat.

The gathering of colors and songs
The solitude of completion
The roundness of finality
The immersion into the Bindu.

------Through concentric circles,
The Bindu expresses the conjunctive journey
Between the inner self and the universe.

A Journey

I lie on the naked sand
Bare, one with the sand
The heaps and the valleys
The undulation of the sand dunes
Reaching the Heavens!

Blanketed in warm shining veil
My every breath massaged by tiny crystals
I lie with God
The golden rays of the red orb
Gently penetrate my pores
My heart, my soul, my spirit

Conveyed on a golden eagle
I soar into the skies and orbit the beyond
Higher and higher, I float
Into Infinity and to Absolute Reality

I touch the face of God
I am caressed by a tender touch
A gentle fold around me takes me yonder
The end is near. Nay. It is Never

In a wakeful sleep, I wander
I wonder and I ponder
How did I get here?
How did I deserve this Beatitude?
Earthbound I was happy
Free now as a wisp of breeze

Never to return, never to wander
A blissful peace prevails.

Immersed into Cosmic Consciousness
I am in *'Shanti Nilaya'* –
The Ultimate home of Peace.

A Shooting Star

Swinging motionless, in midair,
On a blue bridge
Higher and higher
On collision course of Thor
A midnight sojourn, a delectable feast
Invisible friends, all in an airy treat

Winged melody of a million
Imperceptible notes
A million notes
Perceived in a blink
Shimmering, shivering brilliance
Glistening gems far and near
A symphony of highs and lows
Dark and deep, or teasing twinkles

A winged dart, flung skywards
Deeper, a thimble-sized dare
The slanting arrow quivering, piercing
Breaking into another world
Flying into the deep beyond
Slanting, disappearing arrow
'Look, look up, look at me!'

A glorious spark, a brilliant flare
A flaming trail, a shower,
Sprinklings of star-dust
No more!

Launched into a new world
No more of Time!

A Parting Gift

ALL MINDS ARE PART OF ONE
SINGLE CONSCIOUSNESS
- Vedanta Philosophy.
What a beautiful concept!

"They are all alive and well somewhere,
The smallest sprout shows there is really no death,
And if ever there, was it led to forward life,
All goes onward and outward, nothing collapses,
And to die is different from what anyone supposed,
And luckier.
From 'Song of Myself' by Walt Whitman

In SHIVA: The divine energy of dissolution
embodies and entails a Continuity and
Timelessness sometimes. And other times,
spaced in visible time and space.
Life that goes onward and outward, never
collapsing (as Walt Whitman envisioned.)
It dissolves to reappear in another
form; another time.